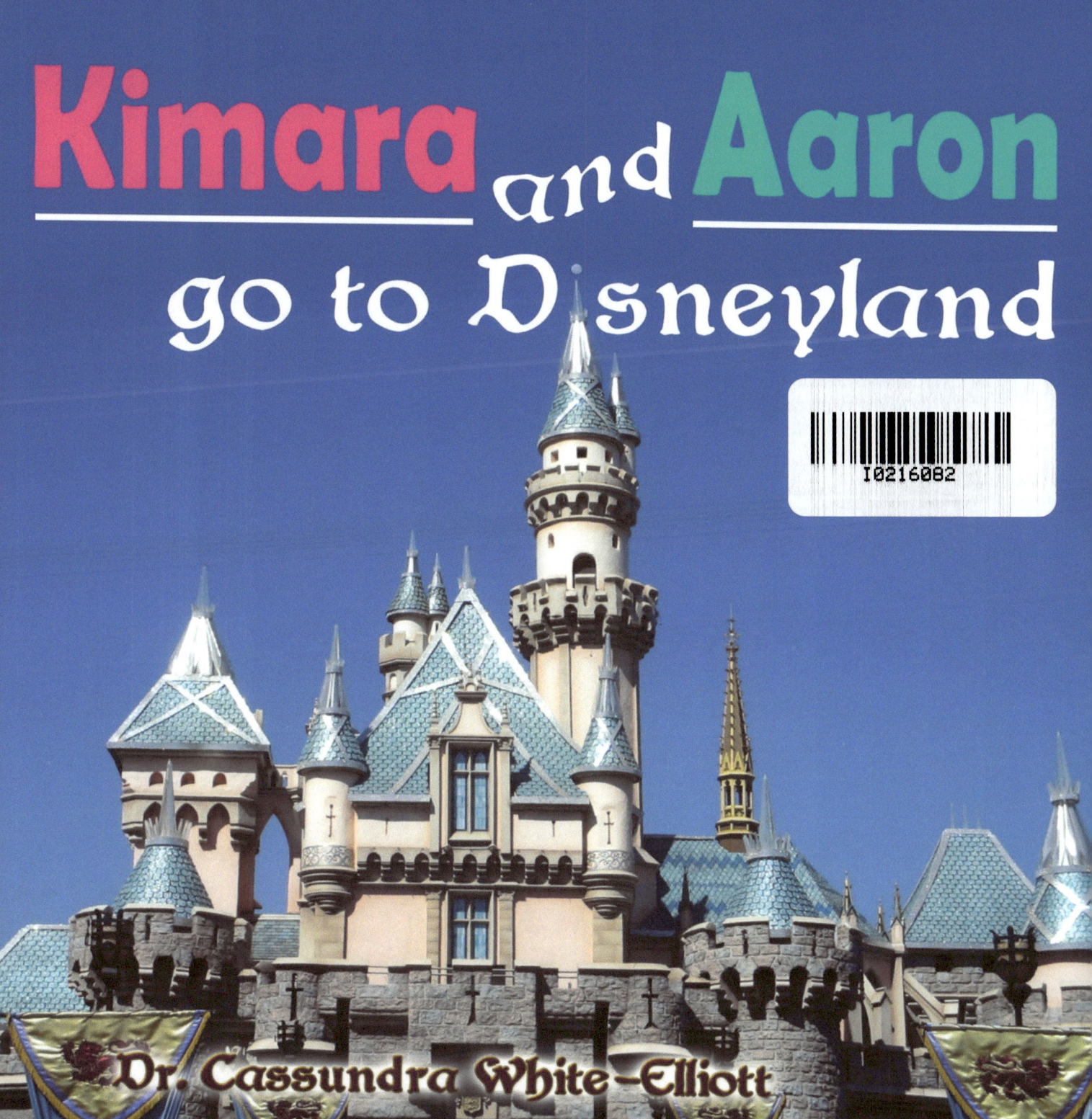

Kimara and Aaron go to Disneyland

Dr. Cassundra White-Elliott

CLF Publishing, LLC.
9161 Sierra Ave, Ste. 203C
Fontana, CA 92335
www.clfpublishing.org

Copyright © 2016 by Cassundra White-Elliott.
All rights reserved.

No portion of this book may be reproduced, stored in a retrieval system, or transmitted by any form or any means electronically, photocopied, recorded, or any other except for brief quotations in printed reviews, without the prior permission of the publisher.

Cover Design by Senir Design. Contact information- info@senirdesign.com.

ISBN # 978-1-945102-11-0

Printed in the United States of America.

This book is dedicated to my two grandloves:

Kimara Tsehai Faith White

and

Aaron Michael White II

In the little city of Barstow, CA, lived two young children: a sister and brother. In Barstow, there isn't much to do, so the two children were always looking for ways to have fun and adventure. Kimara, the oldest of the two children, had a brilliant idea. She knew just the place to go for fun, excitement, and adventure.

On her third birthday, Kimara asked her parents to take her to Disneyland. No luck!

On her fourth birthday, she again asked her parents to take her to Disneyland. No luck!

On her fifth birthday, she still hoped she would wake up on her birthday at Disneyland. Well, no luck yet!

But, for her sixth birthday, things would be different. Kimara's parents and her Nana secretly made plans for a fun-filled adventure inside the Magic Kingdom.

They were finally getting out of Barstow!

Once they arrived and parked the car, the first thing they had to do was ride the shuttle to get inside the theme park. Kimara and Aaron could not stop giggling, because they knew they would soon see where Mickey and Minnie Mouse live.

Inside the park, Kimara and her four-year-old brother Aaron stood on the sidewalk and watched as Minnie, Mickey, and Goofy took pictures with their fans. Suddenly, a marching band came by playing music the kids could dance to.

So, that's exactly what they did!

They danced!

Not too long after, they made their way to one of the most special parts of the park-. It's a Small World! They could have stayed there forever, but, of course, there was so much more to see!

They were amazed by all the different cultures they saw displayed from all over the world.

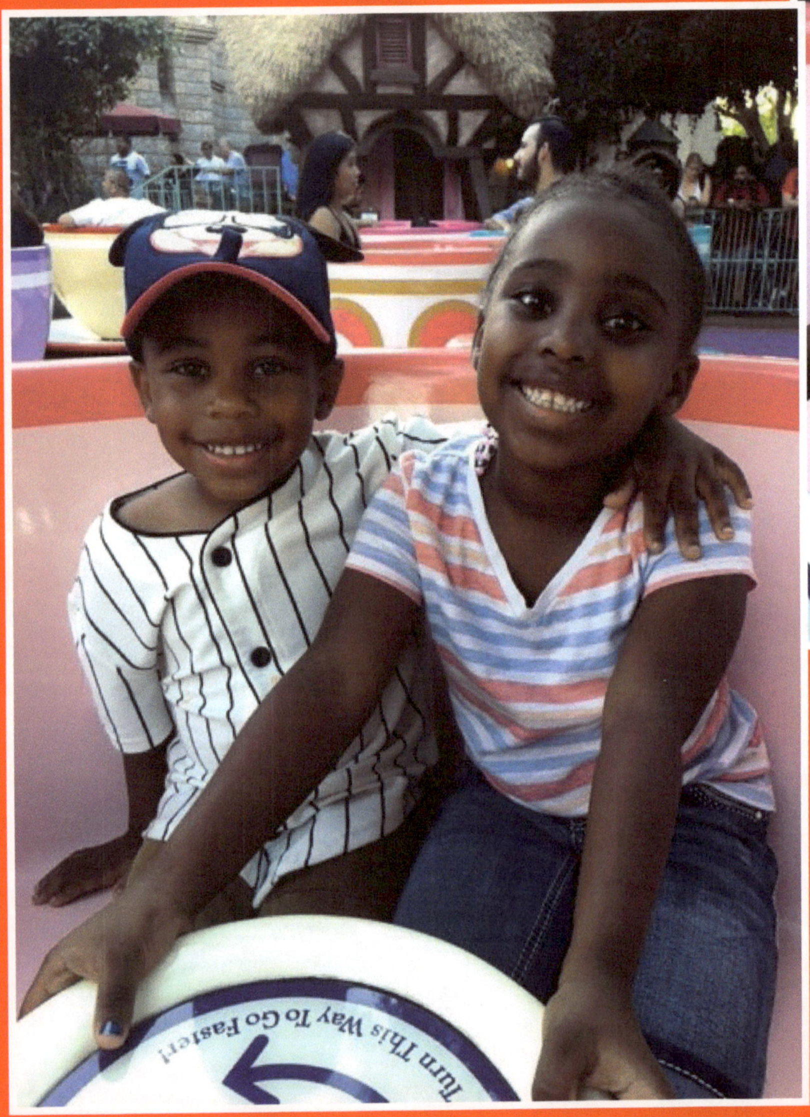
Turn This Way To Go Faster!

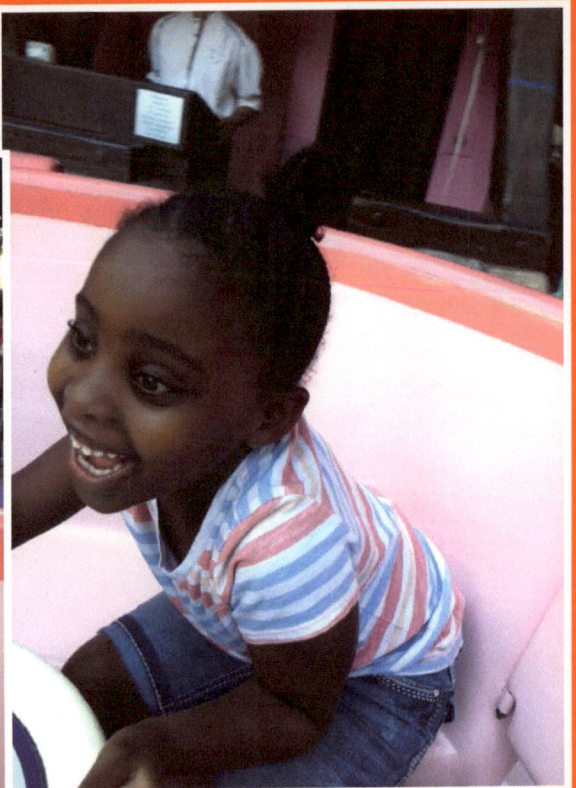

Throughout the day, Kimara and Aaron had a lot of fun. They ate cotton candy and rode so many rides, including the spinning teacups. They took Nana for a ride and spun her around until she was very dizzy and could barely walk straight.

The kids really got a kick out of that!

After three dark and scary rides that almost scared the pants off the children,
Kimara and Aaron decided to take a break from some of the dark indoor rides and took a mellow ride on the
merry-go-round.

What kid can resist that?

Next, off to the Matterhorn!
The family is really having a blast!
Where's Nana?
Oh, she's behind the camera.

Time for the racing, bumper cars!

Kimara rode along with their mother, and Aaron rode along with their father.

Around and around the track they went, bumping into the cars in front and getting bumped from behind.

Watch out! The speed limit is only 50 miles per hour! Slow down!

Woah, good thing there was no police officer there giving tickets....

Kimara and Aaron would have had one for sure!

Disneyland
MONORAIL
MARK VII

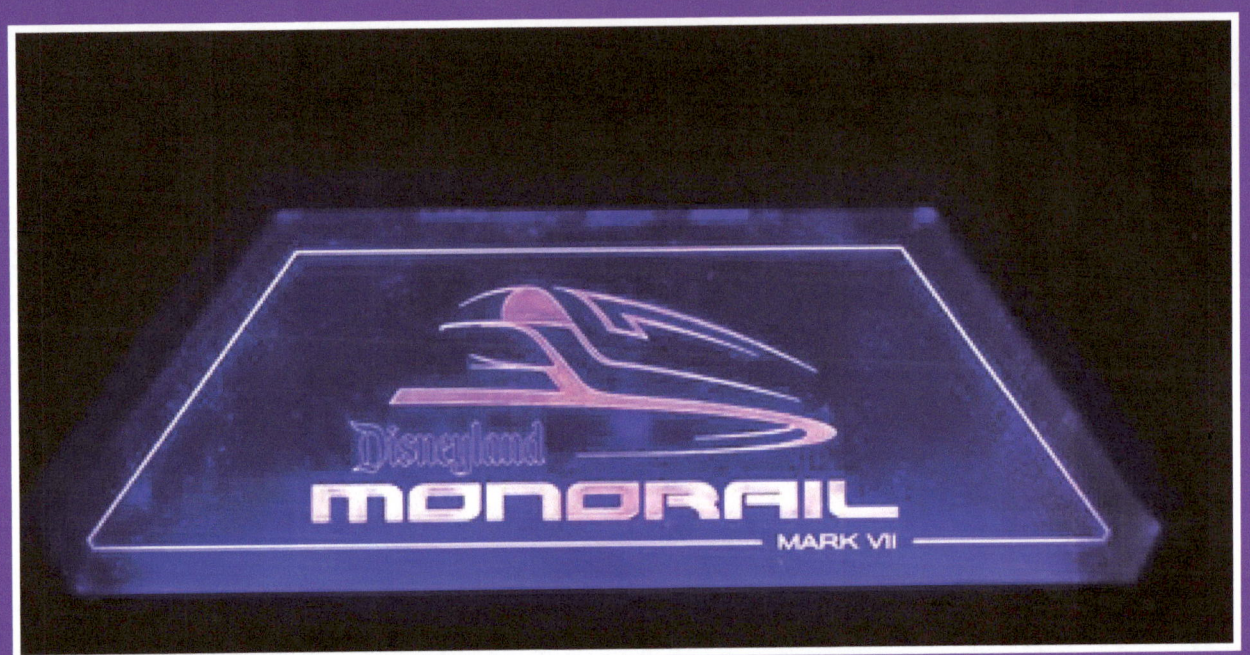

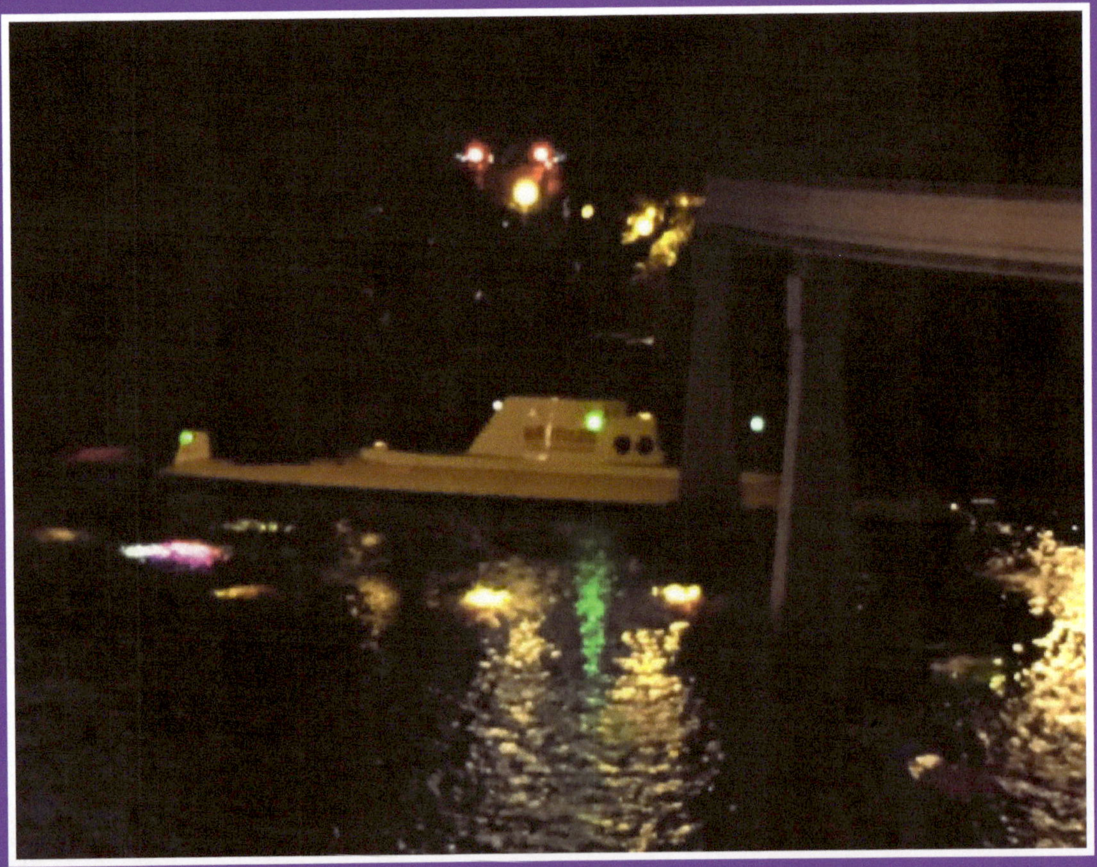

Next, stop- the Monorail and from there, down, down, down, they went- into the yellow submarine to see the marine layers and Nemo, because well...

he was lost of course!

As it grew darker and darker, Kimara and Aaron could not wait to see the fireworks. All of a sudden, they heard a loud noise. They looked up, and in the sky, they saw sparkles of white, red, green, blue, and yellow!

The firework show had begun!

They were gorgeous!

As the night came to a close, they children were satisfied with their adventure to the Magic Kingdom. They found out the Magic Kingdom was truly magical, and I'm sure Kimara wants to spend her seventh birthday there, too.
But, we'll see!

www.ingramcontent.com/pod-product-compliance
Lightning Source LLC
Chambersburg PA
CBHW040032050426
42453CB00002B/86